For the Publisher

Stefan Stevanović
The Secret of Alchemy

The Boy And God's Secret

Stefan Stevanovic and Alchemist

Published by Stefan Stevanovic, 2024.

"The Boy and God's Secret"

Stefan Stevanovic – The Alchemist

❖ AUTHOR'S WORD ❖

This book, along with all its content, I owe to you, Father, who allowed me to realize, and then explain and describe my life and my journey, which is still ongoing. This book is my debt to the world, and it's up to the world whether it will accept or reject it. It's up to each individual soul whether they will embrace these texts and apply them, or perhaps not. You and I know that it is written from a sincere heart, with words of truth, for all the people of this world who face life's unexplainable sufferings, inner battles, and obsessive thoughts, without insight into where it all stems from. And when we don't know the cause, we cannot treat it— for those who ask thousands of questions without the possibility of hearing direct answers, for you always speak— it's only a question of who listens and who is open to receiving your messages, which never cease. My dear readers, if you try to apply the teachings offered in this book, you can expect inevitable results that accompany the process of inner transformation. My goal is to share with you the treasure I was given, not as a gift, but as something that demanded long, exhausting work and time, as well as a special approach to everything we know or thought we knew.

IN THE FIRST BOOK, I have decided to cover only 12 short but thoroughly explained metaphors that Jesus used when addressing humanity, all of which concern their inner application. Each of Jesus' sayings carries deep teachings about self-healing on the spiritual, emotional, and mental levels, leading to the highest state of human consciousness, in which one realizes they are one with everything. Any teaching becomes useless if it cannot be applied in concrete practice—just as it was 2,000 years ago when Jesus existed and spoke, so it is now, in the 21st century.When interpreting and deciphering any kind of sacred text, I had to mentally transport myself back in time to the period in which it was written. Specifically, regarding Jesus, the author mentally takes into account certain factors. These texts were written in a time and environment over 2,000 years ago, and the terminology used then is not the same as it is today. During that time, terms like subconscious, energy, ego, vibration, and frequency did not exist. Therefore, the teachings of that time were conveyed and expressed using the language and concepts of that era and the region where they originated. The author has tried to mentally place himself in that period, when people walked the earth, worked in crafts, cultivated land, and herded sheep. Teachings were mostly passed down from mouth to mouth to ensure their survival, with occasional writings, some of which have reached us today, though perhaps the most important parts were discarded.— "lost in time." But truth always finds its way to those who seek it.

THANK YOU

I am deeply thankful to my beloved, my life's support, who has had and still has the patience and respect for my inner journey, for all the conversations that lasted for hours, where she listened and listened to my discoveries and stories, even when, in the highest states of consciousness, I was sometimes incomprehensible — even to myself, and to her. She guards my necessary moments of silence and shields them from the outside world. You are my witness, the witness of my journey and inner development. I love you.

Thank you to my brother for our conversations on this topic, for the discussions in which we exchanged thoughts on the content of certain scriptures, which helped me in further understanding and sharing this area of interest. The spiritual journey can be, and often is, a lonely process, and support is of great importance. Though we are often far apart, you are always close to my heart. Your brother loves you.

Thank you to my friends who have shared, and continue to share, my highs and lows, and have been there for me whenever needed, each of you on your own life path, dealing with your own challenges.

Thank you to my spiritual brother across the ocean, Daniel Luke-Paulson, with whom I seriously delved into certain topics, who has experienced his personal shipwrecks and yet managed to transform himself.

❖ INTRODUCTION ❖

The Alchemist is ready to share his life with you and all the illusions we are led into, along with the beliefs imposed on us through the passing down of convictions from generation to generation, beginning at birth. It is up to you to accept and embrace the content of this book or to reject it. However, the author advises you to consider these words and reflect on the truths presented in this book. The reason why the author writes about his life in the early pages is primarily to show you the power of transformation that his life embodies, and to highlight that every word in this book has been experienced and tested firsthand.

This book is neither the first nor the last to speak of consciousness, of God, or of the Kingdom of Heaven, but it is one of those that will not judge your life choices. In the author's speech, you might think at times that he criticizes the ways in which we have been given a distorted truth, only to then present it as the only truth—but that is not the case. The author is reconciled with the world around him; he simply uses the method of expression in this book to separate and then reassemble what is effective and applicable from what is not. Truth is multifaceted and liberating, not confined by suppressing everything else, and it comes in many forms.

Just as it is said of Jesus—he does not reveal himself to everyone in the same way; to the poor as a poor man, to the rich as a rich man, to each in the way they can receive the light of truth, in which resides the most beautiful form of human consciousness and the essence of our existence. The author, in writing this content, uses a non-judgmental and gentle tone, aiming to convey these words to your heart and mind, occasionally expressing certain dissatisfactions with the system of life we live in.

Messengers have existed since the beginning of time, and they come in various forms and shapes. God always speaks to man, and if we calm ourselves and open up to the messages surrounding us, we will become true alchemists of inner alchemy. This book has no polarity; it is meant for both men and women, for God in His essence encompasses both. Women have been suppressed and marginalized for centuries, primarily through religions, which, although they use different methods today, still do the same. However, before the face of heaven, WE ARE ALL ONE!

If you ascribe traits and characteristics to God based on "He likes this—He dislikes that," you are still at the beginning of your journey, but that too is not to be condemned. We have all been at the beginning. To avoid waiting life after life, this book will speed up the process of realization and reveal secrets to you, removing the chains from your soul that have bound you since birth. We will strive not to blame or judge anyone. Although, when you discover the truth, those who have hidden it may provoke some form of resentment within you, remain kindhearted toward all that is part of your lives and surroundings. You may wonder why this isn't available to everyone. Are these things being hidden? The world would be a completely different place if even half of this knowledge were presented and propagated instead of what is served to us from the earliest days of life.

We will begin this book with a story from the very beginning—from the author's childhood and life events. The story carries deep emotional pain and permeates his life on all levels, affecting him in a relentless way, but in the end, it becomes part of the great plan of his soul's transformation. Among other things, this journey resulted in the creation of this book, which would not have come to be if the path had not been as it was.

Please forgive any potential mistakes you may find in the text, as this is an amateur work, the first public presentation of this piece, with the goal of understanding the content of true importance, rather than focusing on the handwriting style, which will, of course, remain within the domain of understandable reading. Perhaps one day, if necessary, it will also take on a professional edition.

The author shares all these texts with you, typing away with his fingers on the keyboard, opening his life and heart to you with the hope that you will realize you are a great light and that you are always loved, regardless of the environment and situations life brings your way.

⎯⎯⎯◉⎯⎯⎯

❖ LIFE EXPERIENCES AND BELIEFS ❖

Growing Up and Acquiring Wrong Beliefs

When I was very young, growing up was quite difficult. I was raised with beliefs that were promoted then, as they are now, by religious communities. These beliefs revolved around the idea that we must be extremely humble and submissive toward everything, that we were conceived in some form of sin, and as such, created a type of physical separation from God. We were taught that we must bow to external buildings, and that there's no problem — God is one and above, while we are something else entirely and below. There was also this inner guidance that we should disdain this world and avoid attachment to material things, which today, even outside of religious circles, are often considered the root of all evil.

But if you hold a knife (material things) in your hand, will you harm someone with it, or will you use it to cut bread and serve it to others? The knife itself is not the root of evil, but a tool; how we choose to use it is up to us, right? We were taught to seek salvation solely in external institutions, to endure and tolerate all the negativity of life, to swallow it down and suffer. Once in a while, typically once a week, we would head towards lavish palaces where God is supposedly only present.I now see those places as exclusively places of peace due to the energetic presence of prayer and the surroundings that are far from the population; places of peace that occasionally do good for a person. However, our natural habitat is our body; if you do not find peace within it, you will not find it anywhere else. It is the temple of our souls, yet the belief that we all carry some family curses and that it must be so—because we all originated in sin and are here to suffer—cannot support all those palaces that claim to know God better than anyone else. Our God turns out to be a jealous God who needs our money and will condemn us to eternal fire where we will burn and our souls will be scorched, where we will suffocate for eternity, yet He LOVES us UNCONDITIONALLY! That some of us are His while others are not, thus making us better and them worse. One day, when we leave, we will be happy, but of course only when we leave this place, all

---

IN THE NAME OF THE greatest Divine soul that ever existed, whom no one wanted or desired to understand—Jesus. But alright, everything is as it is.

Considering such a kind of upbringing, I began to accept these beliefs as absolute truths. I myself grew up in a very humble family where money was only used for the basic needs of the family, where it was often very difficult to survive, and there were many moments when even basic needs were not met. My parents, whom I do not blame at all because I know how hard they fought to prevent such things from happening, spent their entire lives going in circles, but it was all without success. Although they had jobs and were not people who wasted money on unnecessary things.

My family — my mom, my mom's mom, my dad, my brother, and I — consisted of five members, and with modest income, it was extremely hard to survive and fulfill all our childhood desires and needs. Needs were fulfilled with great difficulty, while desires often had to wait for a long time.

Because of this upbringing and the literal interpretation of the beliefs I was given, it was fatal for my future way of life, but I still didn't realize it. I had already firmly embraced the belief that spirituality and the material world could never coexist. Being inclined towards spirituality since i could remember, and having nurtured a great love for God as the Creator, I imagined He would condemn every attempt of mine to strive towards the material. Yet, deep inside, I longed to break free from the chains of poverty. However, since it was incompatible with my beliefs, I chose not to strive for, and to reject and deny my desire for the material world, which had always been within me, secretly distressing and draining me from the inside.

Why did we come here, after all? To condemn all this and then leave, while certain communities grow rich by offering and repeating the same stories for decades, which they themselves do not fully understand. Short-lived, words remedies accompanied by certain forms of paganism like, "Turn around three times, and you'll lift the curse and sin," guiding us to look outward when everything we need is within us, right before our eyes. In the meantime, we are always the ones to blame and suffer, because of Adam and Eve, because of our grandfather, great-grandfather, great-great-grandfather, and so on.because they couldn't offer a concrete answer or solution. To be able to, they would first have to understand themselves, and that is a path and process not taught in schools. Life steers you in that direction when you nurture it within yourself and when you strive to understand something deeper than the illusions of the world in front of you. Jesus said, "Seek and you will find, knock and it will be opened to you." Of course, this is not meant in a material sense. This isn't a millionaire mentor's guide, but rather, it's about our essence, the core part of us stripped to the bone, what remains when everything else falls away.

I was 7 years old when school started, and my first days were somewhat pleasant. But soon, due to the lack of finances, I felt ashamed to show up at school in torn sneakers or wearing clothes that weren't quite right for me — either too big, borrowed, or not fitting properly for a child. Years went by, and my mother had to take severance pay and leave her job. With part of that money, she invested in starting a small business at a market stall in the city. There was some activity, and at that time, selling cigarettes under the table could be done cautiously to avoid getting caught by the police.

Many winter days, I spent at the stall, offering support to my parents. Business wasn't going well. We somehow got stuck with a stall that was available, but it wasn't in a prime spot; it was at the far end of the market, where few people ever ventured. The issues with sales continued, so we tried selling cigarettes on the side in the city center during the afternoons. I fully joined in that effort,

Although my parents resisted, I insisted on being involved. That's how I started selling on my own. I took a box, cut it, and made a holder for cigarettes that I carried in my hand. Since I was a small, chubby boy with a sweet face, people chose to buy from me, which caused some frowns from other vendors, but I was happy about it. There was a bit more money at home, and things felt lighter. This lasted for about 2-3 years.

After that, due to new laws, we had to return to selling only at the market stall. My dad's job at the paint and lacquer factory, where he worked day and night, not knowing when he was working or when he wasn't, led to his physical and mental deterioration. Mom struggled at the market stall due to poor sales, and Dad at the factory, losing track of time altogether. As a boy, I remained cheerful despite all this. My brother and I went through all these events together and experienced them in similar ways internally. This kind of upbringing can be very hard on children and leave deep scars, creating so many internal blocks that it can truly be detrimental to their future lives.

We spent a lot of time on the streets, picking up various behavior patterns from different people around us—some useful, some not—and yes, we saw a lot for our age. While other kids had family environments and created school memories, we were living a different side of life.

School was a disaster, both for me and my brother. Skipping school, driven by the fear of humiliation and judgment due to our material shortcomings and the beliefs surrounding us, affected our school days. The teacher always said we were very intelligent and that there was another issue, that it was a great shame we didn't apply ourselves to school. I know there are children who, even in the deepest poverty, become the greatest doctors and scientists, but we were preoccupied with achieving financial stability, so we did all kinds of useful things on the street to earn money. I remember once buying sunflower seeds, roasting them at home, making paper cones, and going to sell them in front of the cinema. I recall the well-dressed guys with their girlfriends and the scents of perfumes I had never smelled before, thinking, "Ah, just a moment of that beautiful fragrance of life in my nostrils." I have to admit, the sunflower seeds weren't that great; I didn't wait long enough,i run to my home, they were a bit over-roasted — laugh — but I consoled myself, thinking at least my intentions were honorable — laugh.

I came home with not much money earned, but maybe enough for a soda, some snacks, and gum, which was enough to make me happy at that moment.

At the time, I was fascinated by the cinema. I would often stand in front of the movie theater's billboards and see what was playing that evening. Every afternoon, I'd go there to look at what was on the screen and watch the people entering the hall. These seemingly ordinary, regular people appeared to me as special individuals in the glow of the cinema's lobby light, which made everyone feel a little important — or at least that's how it seemed to me back then.

I became friends with the popcorn seller, who sold popcorn outside the cinema every evening, and one thing was for sure — every night, you could always find me, a little boy, standing by the entrance and her, the popcorn seller. Over time, she opened up to me, telling me stories from her life and sharing what was going on in her world, while I mostly talked about childish things — after all, I was about 10 years old at the time. I was fortunate to get the occasional free bag of popcorn during those evening hours.

I often thought about sneaking past the guard to watch a movie, and I remember one night, after thinking about it for a while, I managed to do it. That same evening, it felt like I was infiltrating one of the most secure buildings in the world, and it seemed like everyone in the hall knew exactly how I had gotten in.

Finally, the first movie — me and the screen in front of me, darkness... the film begins. A few times, the popcorn seller managed to let me in, and that's when I got to watch some of my first films. The effort of waiting outside the cinema every evening paid off.

I always believed that I would find a way to get inside, and there it was, it happened. That period of my life always brings up strange memories for me, a mix of sentimentality and sadness, but that's all part of life, isn't it?

❖ Grandma Dies - Moving - New Beginnings ❖

Grandma died from heart problems. Unfortunately, that moment could not pass without my involvement in everything. I was at home, she was there, and we were alone. My parents were at work, and my brother was somewhere in school, as far as I remember. I heard a groan from the room and went inside. I saw Grandma slowly starting to fade away, clutching her chest. At that point, I already knew I needed to give her nitroglycerin under her tongue, the tablet she kept with her for such reasons. I saw she was in pain, and I hurried to place the tablet under her tongue while she was writhing in agony. I watched the scene in fear, trying to do something. Confused, I called for an ambulance, explained the situation, and ran around, not knowing what to do. The ambulance arrived very quickly and took her to the hospital,in which she passed away after a few days. The family was very sad, and the atmosphere was gloomy for days. That strange air of death filled the space.

My grandmother had two small apartments in the city. We lived in one, and the other was rented out to a tenant who had been leasing it from her. My parents rarely had help from others in their lives, except when my father had to lower his head and go borrow money for us or to humble himself and listen to lectures, so he could ultimately buy necessities with the money from Grandma. Grandma generally did not support their marriage from the very beginning until the end of her life because he was a man from the countryside, and she was a city girl, and in her opinion, she should have married someone much better.

When Grandma died, my parents started to think that if we sold both apartments, we could pay off all our debts and build a big house on my father's property, where we would all have enough space to live without crowding. The apartments were very small, and the best solution at that moment was that new beginning — in a big house, with a large yard, and with the peace of mind that after years of debt, we could sleep more soundly and have enough space to separate and have our own private space.

The apartments were sold very quickly — first one, then the other. The house began to be built rapidly and was successfully completed. It was a period I had dreamed of — financial security and fulfilling childhood wishes without delays and waiting, as had been the case before. They really made an effort to ensure we had everything at that moment.

❖ New Home-New Beginning-Fall ❖

After the house was nearly finished, my father's brother-in-law joined our lives, to whom I won't dedicate more words than necessary. In short, with some promises to secure a future for me and my brother, based on the great trust and kindness of my father, he pulled a large amount of money from us and vanished in the blink of an eye. The tower began to crumble, and with it, our lives. A period of struggle followed, aside from the daily details that were unfolding — a struggle that had returned to our home, that dark cloud of poverty that once again enveloped me and my family. This time, even further from the city, in a large unfinished house by the river, with a view of the forest and an unfriendly environment, except for a few people who occasionally appeared.

Now, with no possibility for further advancement, we were left in an unfinished house that lacked electricity, water, a bathroom, or a fenced yard. At that time, I was 16 years old and was already trying to find extra ways to earn money, but far from the city and the happenings,

it was very difficult. I lost my friends from the neighborhood, and I hadn't made new ones yet. I was alone and spent most of my days in my room, thinking and often crying over the events that had resurfaced in our lives, even though we thought we had escaped them forever.

Faith in people and their promises took its toll, leading to the collapse of my life and the lives of my family. A question arose: should we even trust people? God was always with me; I always felt His presence, but still held the belief that it was against Him for me to be a child who could be completely happy. I regarded my desires as even more wrong after this experience. My beliefs were further reinforced that God demanded just that — precisely that life in such an environment for us, to save us from some unknown sins, and that a secure place awaited us in the promised paradise when it all comes to an end.

In such situations, a person might think about doing something to themselves and their life to reach that promised paradise as quickly as possible, because there lies the promise — over there, somewhere, not here. This is how people have passed down beliefs from generation to generation. Wait... did I say people? Yes, people, just like you and me — only people with certain titles and a dress code, so they seemed wise. But were they really? What if they misunderstood? After all, that is their perception of things, and Jesus clearly tells us to examine the face of heaven and earth,to examine until we find our truth.

It would be right to reassess things — if the recipe has not borne fruit for thousands of years, then you must study the recipe again to acknowledge mistakes and see where the errors arose in the interpretation of the recipe, in the perception of the one interpreting it, and to admit the mistake while striving for the truth. However, this is not so difficult, especially when you are a mediator between God and people; it becomes even easier to admit a mistake because you have insights into profound matters and teachings that are inaccessible to others, or is it so hard to acknowledge that we may have erred somewhere in history in our interpretation? Or will we cling to something as a drunkard clings to a fence, believing it's impossible for us to make a mistake, but for others, yes — not for us! It's better to eat tasteless food for thousands of years than to admit to ourselves and to the people-nations that we might have been wrong and to acknowledge it, as we strive for love and it's important for us to collectively improve ourselves for the betterment of humanity.

Or perhaps you leave everything as it is — after all, is fear not beneficial in the end? It doesn't really matter; some genuinely don't know but learn and pass on this hidden treasure, some know but are powerless, while others know and do not want to change anything. However, in this book and those that follow, we will see what we ought to do

❖ **Natural Expression of Deep Faith in Oneself** ❖

I was around 17 years old, and I had made some new friends and formed some new friendships in that environment. Among them were friends who were not particularly well-meaning toward me, but I had two good buddies. One of them shared all the good and bad moments in my family with me. He was like a member of my family, and I was like a member of his small family as well. We often spent days at his place or mine, talking about the good things that life can offer. It was a friendship in which we shared life stories, problems, our home, and food at the table — a solid friendship where we often supported each other, devising plans for the businesses we could run in the future.

I was at that age when you think you can do anything, but I was quite blocked by beliefs from my youth, yet I had a strong subconscious faith in myself. I remember one time when we were sitting at my place. I told him, "Sale, I want to buy a car," to which he replied, "Okay, but you don't have any money. Do you have any money? Did you get something?" I said, "No, but I want to buy a car." I grabbed the classifieds, opened them, and started looking for a car. He looked at me strangely and said again, "Brother, you don't have money. Where and how do you think you'll buy a car? What's your plan?" I replied once more, "I'm buying a car today, and that's how it will be. I don't know how, but I will buy it."

At that moment, I didn't even know what was happening to me that day and what was subconsciously going on within me. I searched, flipped through many ads, and called about one ad for a car that I really liked: "Good day, I'm calling about the car ad. Is it still valid?" The man on the other end replied, "Yes, of course, the ad is active." I told him I would come with my friend to look at the car in about an hour. My friend still thought I was crazy for even doing this, but since we weren't doing anything special anyway, he took it as: "Okay, let's go for a ride."

We arrived at the house. The owner came out and warmly greeted us. I sat down and took a drive around the neighborhood, confirming that I liked everything. I returned and told the seller that I really liked the car and that I wanted to buy it. Just as I was about to say that I needed a few days to get the money, he interrupted me and invited us into his home for a drink. We went inside, and while we talked about how reliable the car was and the things that might need investment, he suddenly got up and said, "Come with me, I'll show you something behind the house.

We started walking, and I looked at a brand-new white car behind his house; it looked beautiful, just like something from a showroom. He continued, "You see, I won this car a few days ago in a Bingo lottery. I want you to take my old car and drive it away; you don't have to pay me now. You can give me the money when you have it." We were shocked, and I was so grateful. I got into my new car and drove home.

In this story, the power of faith in oneself and in God is revealed. Out of hundreds of ads, I happened to find that one, and everything unfolded exactly as I wanted. It was my first time, but not the last. Later, using this knowledge, I overcame many life obstacles. For the first time, I saw what belief in oneself and the universe can do. It was more profound and stronger than mere faith; it was absolute knowledge that I was going to go and get what I wanted, regardless of the external circumstances I've described and continue to describe.

❖ Sorrow-Loss-Death-Loneliness ❖

I skipped a few years, and now I am 19 years old. To avoid prolonging stories about daily struggles, temptations, frequent tears, constant worries, with an occasional day of genuine happiness and very rare moments of the same, preparing for New Year or a celebration was a real challenge for my family. It was all one enchanted circle of my life, in which I mostly shared my days with God. You know what? I still share them; it's always been him and me.

In my family, there was always support for one another, tolerance, and respect. My father was my best friend, a truly good and honest being, my greatest support. My mother was a true lion in spirit and heart, a great fighter and a woman with whom I would have coffee as if she were my best friend. There was little feeling of parental authority, yet she was respected. We were such great friends, before being father and son or mother and child, that it made me always, even today, hold family as a great significance in front of me — but not just family as a name, but what it embodies: mutual support, love, respect.

In the same yard, in a small house next to ours, lived my grandmother, my father's mother. That year, she suddenly fell ill, and with her attitude that she neither needed nor wanted a doctor, after all possible pressure, the moment came when it was too late even for the doctor. I spent her last hours by her bedside, and my dad was there. The time for her departure to that promised paradise had come, and my father and I went through every step of her preparation for that journey. With my own hands, I helped my dad dress her and pack her into the small cabinet where we all eventually lay down. It was very hard for me, as a young guy, a very traumatic situation, filled with tears and the deep pain of my father, as well as ourselves — always alone, in all life circumstances, relying only on ourselves. I wanted to show my strength, that I was there for my family, and I jumped in to help and do this because, after all, she is my grandmother, and she deserved it. It was truly painful, and once again, a dark wave loomed over our lives. After the funeral, when I lay somewhere between wakefulness and sleep, she came to me and cuddle my cheek.

I felt, in a literal sense, her hand passing over my face; I admit, fear began to overwhelm me. I felt her gratitude and love because I bore that burden that was not at all light. That loss was still ongoing, for not even a year had passed when my mother one day began to feel internal pain and was not well. The doctors diagnosed her with gallbladder issues and stated that she needed surgery. The surgery followed, she was released home, but her health remained poor. Later, they informed my dad that she also had a tumor on her pancreas and that it was a matter of days. Another shock. I had already turned 20; due to my grandmother's death, we celebrated very moderately.

Mom was at home, taking strong painkillers, often unconscious, the therapies were too strong — morphine and Trodon were the main medications. Dad had to work, so I took on many responsibilities. Every day, I was at home with her, caring for her, slowly leading her to the bathroom, feeding her, and washing her.

A painful morning dawned; Dad was entering the house after the night shift. I was lying beside her, sleeping, because I wanted her to always have the necessary care. I heard her breaths, which were very strange, I heard some rough sigh coming from her lungs, as if something was scraping inside her. The night before, she had lowered my head into her lap and said: — My son, my angel, thank you for everything. Remember, son, we have no one else but ourselves. — Those sighs sent chills over me; Dad began to cry.

We stood beside her, and within a few minutes, her breathing completely stopped. It was over. We all gathered around her, pain, sorrow, and tears overwhelmed Dad, my brother, and me. It hurt deeply;

we always had each other, if nothing else. I helped Dad prepare Mom, putting on her jacket; I slipped a bill into her bag and placed it in the small cabinet that would take her on her journey to the promised paradise, which had presumably finally led her out of that vicious cycle of life. The day of the funeral arrived. Dad and my brother went to prepare everything to honor the customs. We were all broken. Dad was dying of grief, choking on tears and pain, but everything had to be done. My brother was falling apart inside from everything that was happening. I sat beside her, noticing red fluid leaking from her nostrils, mouth, and ears. I ran for a towel to wipe her face; I didn't want her to be remembered differently. I wiped her face every 15 minutes; I don't even need to mention what I was going through inside. In the end, we decided, of course, that the cabinet would remain closed for obvious reasons. Although a few months prior, we had given Grandma a year from her death; we had to relive everything again. Now there were only three of us left, in less than a year.

❖ Dad-Brother-Me ❖

My brother went to work by the seaside in other country called Montenegro, where he had worked for years. He returned to earn some money because finances had always been our challenge and a painful point. Dad worked at the same company as before, and I helped around the house. At that time, we decided it was best for someone to stay at home and take on the responsibilities since Mom passed away on December 23, 2010.

Step by step, Dad and I encouraged each other; we spent a lot of time together when he was free, functioning as one soul. We comforted each other, cried, and supported one another. I stayed in regular contact with my brother, and he helped us during that period. I always tried to ensure that when Dad came home, there was fresh bread, warm food, and coffee on the table. I knew how to do all of that and had learned it well.

In those months, I met and started writing to a girl who was living in Vienna, Austria at the time. She somehow brightened my soul and made me laugh when that was truly impossible. We spent nights writing and talking over Skype. It felt like God had sent her into my life, as at that time, very few, almost no one, would knock on the door to see how we were doing, except for two friends who would come by.

Those conversations and calls were my shining moments. I really liked her, but I often thought about what I could offer this girl beyond our virtual conversations and writing. I lived in a pretty tough financial situation, in an unstable home—not exactly something girls want to hear or see. Yet, she was there. She didn't give up on me; every free moment of hers and mine was filled with long conversations.

Somewhere around the end of November 2011, about 11 months after my mother's death, Dad had a leg fracture at work. While he was resting at home, I took care of him, but he got worse. He began to complain about a sore throat and couldn't swallow well. Since the situation seemed a bit serious, even though it lasted only 3-4 days, we went to the doctor. The doctors examined him, looked into it, thought it was viral, and gave various diagnoses, but the blood test showed that something more serious was present—a throat cancer in an advanced stage, which had been present for months, but since his immune system was strong and he was active, it hadn't manifested.

More precisely, it arose due to a drop in his immunity, which happened because of the leg fracture. One afternoon, he felt so bad that I called an ambulance, which arrived after an hour and took us to the hospital. While the doctors examined him, I heard them mumbling and whispering, and Dad and I assumed they would keep him in the hospital because he needed care and strong pain medication. Instead, the doctor came out and told me, "Your father will be fine. Just stop by and get him some painkillers, and go home; everything will be alright. He doesn't need to stay in the hospital." I was in shock. Despite my explanations of the situation and my pleas, nothing changed. Dad could hardly speak and was very weak. I pushed him in a wheelchair and went to get the doctor to prescribe an additional antibiotic along with the painkillers.

While i was waiting outside the door, I called my uncle, whom i rarely hear from, but who has always been there for us. He is a great expert, highly regarded and respected. I tried to seek his help for Dad, asking for him to be admitted to the hospital. He called the doctor next to whom i was standing at the moment she was writing the prescription. She instantly changed everything, threw away the written prescriptions, and called for an ambulance to take us to the chest department for him to be admitted there. We went there and encountered some resistance, under the pretext that there was no room, but we managed anyway. He stayed in the hospital, and I returned home alone.

I cant describe all those things, all those emotions, and all the internal happenings within me, but the hell on earth was like the culmination of everything from my childhood, like a seal at the end of the paper of life experiences. We were writing messages back and forth; he was very concerned about me. I visited him every day and gave him water soaked with my fingers because he was very thirsty. Each sip caused him to react by hitting his foot against the side of the bed from the pain. He told me it was time for him to go and feared for me.

In the meantime, I was updating the girl I was dating about the events in my life. She was always there for me, to comfort me and provide support. This was immeasurably significant to me at those moments when I no longer knew what, where, or how. One day, Dad stopped responding to my text messages. I went to the hospital and saw the empty bed, but I secretly thought he had been transferred. A nurse met me and directed me to the doctor, who, in very cold and brief terms, told me: "Well, you know what, he has passed away." I ran out of the hospital and headed in an unknown direction, step by step, not knowing where I was going or what I was doing. It took a long time for me to realize where I was. Darkness fell, and then I called myself back and knew that I had to do my job and prepare everything for the journey to that promised paradise. The girl was my maximum support, and Dad's company helped me with the funeral costs. But again, I had to enter a room full of people who were no longer alive and identify my dad. Even today, I don't know why I did it in such detail. I looked at once strong hands that now looked like a child's and a hollow face, a tired man, worn out from life and illness. And I had God's strength to endure all of that and consciously carry out everything for that journey.

The date was December 3, 2011. On December 23, I was supposed to prepare for my mother's one-year death anniversary, but before that, I had to send my father on his own journey. My brother came, barely managing, as he was tied down by work and survival, to be with me during those days.

In the end, we agreed that he had to go back because we couldn't afford to lose everything. I had to get back on my feet and secure our situation, and he would be a great help in that. We couldn't both fall.

I remember the moment when I closed the front door and found myself completely alone. Our relatives lived all around us, but they probably didn't feel the need or the urge to check on the boy who was left alone in that house. I don't need to explain what was happening inside me – the emotions, feelings, thoughts, sorrow, suffering, and pain after everything that had happened. At one point, I started to scream out loud. Even today, I can't fully explain that situation in my mind, but I addressed God, as if talking to someone I know well from my surroundings: "YOU KNOW BEST! WE'VE BEEN TOGETHER MY WHOLE LIFE, I CARRY YOU IN EVERY MOMENT OF MY LIFE AS MY BEST FRIEND, BUT I WANT TO KNOW! I NEED TO KNOW WHY THIS HAPPENS, WHY PEOPLE GO THROUGH SUCH THINGS?""WHY IS THIS HAPPENING? EXPLAIN IT TO ME, I DON'T WANT SILENCE! I WANT A VOICE, I WANT TO KNOW!!! I DON'T WANT OTHERS TO TELL ME, I WANT YOU TO TELL ME! I'M NOT INTERESTED IN PRIESTS OR INSTITUTIONS BUILT IN YOUR NAME; I WANT TO HEAR YOUR VOICE!!!"

I had to stay rational because I needed to prepare for my mother's one-year death anniversary on December 23. No job, no money, just my life ahead of me—living on like that was going to be quite a challenge, wasn't it?

❖ A Few Years Later ❖

In the meantime, the girl who had been my greatest support during those difficult times came to Serbia. After spending three days together, I got a job offer at the coast, so I went there. She joined me after a few days, and we started living together. Yet another difficult beginning, full of challenges, was ahead of us. The job wasn't great, and it felt like we were just going in circles, but in those challenges, we swam together and somehow managed to be happy, even though surviving on the coast was stressful. We had the option to separate until the season ended, but we chose not to part at any cost, deciding that from now on, we would face everything together.

Three days of shared moments were enough for us to start living together, and now, 12 years later as I write this, we are still going strong.

We had so much to go through and overcome. When we returned from the coast, we didn't know where we would live because we hadn't saved any money from the season. Since we had been paying for private accommodation throughout the season just to stay together, we were working merely to survive. The house was in poor condition, but we started our life there, living under conditions that felt like they were from the previous century. Somehow, we managed to stay afloat despite the hardships and the lack of basic living conditions. I took on temporary jobs, and it was difficult to earn enough money.

Then one day, the nausea started, and we found out she was pregnant – a huge moment of joy! Right until the end, we didn't know the baby's gender, but that didn't matter to either of us. We were simply happy because a child is a child, and it would be loved no matter what. We never burdened ourselves with those kinds of expectations.

Then came the call from the hospital. She called her mom and said, "Tell Stefan I gave birth to Dragana." That was my mother's name, and I was overwhelmed with emotion. She carried the name of her grandmother. In moments like that, you feel a mix of happiness, sadness, joy, and fear – happiness for the new life of a little girl who would carry her grandmother's name, sadness because her grandparents wouldn't be able to live through and share this joy with me, joy because everything had turned out well, and fear because of the uncertainty of how we would manage and prepare for everything. The only new outfit for Dragana, for her to leave the hospital, was all we had.

These are great struggles that perhaps certain readers of this book may not fully grasp, and thousands of questions might arise as to why certain decisions were made or why things weren't done differently. However, every life experience and its environment are unique, and what I have come to realize is that each present moment is preceded by many moments before it, leading to a particular larger moment.

❖ JESUS AND THE DREAM – The Beginning of the Search ❖

That day, I stood in front of the icons on the shelves in our home, among them a crucifix depicting the crucifixion of Jesus. Standing before it, I opened my heart as I never had before and asked, "God, Jesus, I have always wanted to know more, to know You, to know God, to know how to be truly happy within myself, here and now while I am alive. Is that even fully possible? I want to know You, I want to know everything about You while I am alive, I want to know it all. I want to break life down into the tiniest pieces and understand myself, who I am, what all this is, and why. What is the purpose, what lies behind this stage called life? I am ready to face any truth, even if people call me crazy. I want You to tell me everything because I want to know!"

That moment stirred emotions in me that I had never felt before. A love for Jesus and the love I had for the Creator had always been prominent within me, as I had walked with Him my entire life, hand in hand, both in my mind and heart. After that moment, I returned to reality, but the feeling of that lived moment left a lasting mark on me. That night, I fell asleep, and the dream came.

I stood on Golgotha, the place of Jesus' crucifixion, looking up at the great cross, just like the one depicted in films, and there was Jesus. I looked at Him, nailed to the cross, and He was looking straight into my eyes. I watched as He took His last breath on the cross, His body wounded and stained with blood, the crown of thorns cruelly placed on His head, and the spear wound near His heart. As He exhaled His final breath and closed His eyes, which had been fixed on mine, the sky and earth came together, just like I had seen in movies as a child, filled with awe and sorrow. Thunder roared, lightning flashed, and everything around was shaking, but I stood there, motionless, beneath Him, watching. At no moment did I feel fear or anything similar; I was simply an observer.

Suddenly, a white circle of light appeared in the sky, and He appeared again, descending from that circle of light, directly in front of me, completely unscathed, in His traditional robe from that time. He placed His hand on my shoulder. Though He didn't speak a single word, I felt an unimaginable love, a love that I would feel again several years later.about which I will speak later. That love, that indescribable feeling, something unimaginable, not of this world, which only God can give — that unconditional love and sense of complete peace — remained etched into me just like that dream. From that moment on, everything began, and I started receiving insights. From that dream onwards, it was as if I was being guided by some inner voice towards the beginning of my journey of self-discovery and situations I never thought I would encounter.

❖ In the Meantime, Another Child ❖

Life Triumphs Over Death

I want to quickly get to the interpretations that will resonate with you in this book, but I cannot skip over the part of life where birth replaced death. I'll try to keep it brief but still convey what is important. I won't often return to my life in this book or the ones that will follow, as the essence is laid out before you. What you have before you is an ordinary man with a difficult life story, someone just like you—not a university-educated person who has read it all and now rewrites it, but someone who has personally lived through everything they write about. I bring you all the events from my life.

Every December 3rd and December 23rd felt like ruins to me. Those two days in the year were always particularly hard for me because the memories of my parents became even more vivid, along with everything I had gone through.

When my wife became pregnant for the second time, and they established that the conception date was February 23rd (my father's birthday), I was in shock, overwhelmed by emotions. When we reconfirmed this and the doctor also confirmed the date, my heart was filled with an indescribable warmth. My wife had many personal health complications during the pregnancy, and things didn't go as smoothly as we had hoped—there were many challenges. As the due date, November 29th, approached, we were all excited about welcoming new life into our home.

November came, but there were no signs that the baby would be born. Then something magical and miraculous happened, a moment that made it crystal clear that I had received a message, pure and obvious, from the world from which we all originate—a world that is our true home, a place we always return to. This world is the source we come from and to which we depart every moment. On December 2nd, my wife's water broke. She was ready for labor for over 12 hours, and the anticipation was palpable. The birth finally happened on December 3rd! (The date of my father's death!) It happened exactly on the night of December 3rd at 2:33 a.m.—life replaced death!

The baby was conceived on the day of my father's birthday and born on the day of his death. Even the time of birth, 2:33, is numerologically incredible, as it can be divided into February 23rd and December 3rd. Numbers play a significant role here, as does the sequence of events. The age gap between the first and second child is exactly nine years.

How could I now look at December 3rd with sadness? How could I feel sorrow on my child's birthday when that day has now become a day of birth and celebration of life? I am infinitely grateful to God, because communication is two-way. Along with the insights into life's mysteries that He has provided by elevating my consciousness to the level of divine emotions, He also showed me on the physical plane how my connection to the Heavenly Father has been seen and followed, along with all the events in my life.

Let's be clear: I am always grateful—for happiness, for sorrow, for joy, and for pain. I am thankful for every fall I have experienced and endured in life. Ever since I came to know the Father and the Creator, since I have come to know myself, I know who I am and what I am, who we are and what we are. I understand causes and consequences. No one will ever mislead this child again. I am thankful for everything that has happened because I wouldn't be who I am today if I hadn't endured all the suffering I went through. But the point is this: if I can do it, so can you. That's why I have laid out my life before getting into all that I will write about—about life, the Heavenly Father, the kingdom of heaven, the causes of suffering, and overcoming it, about alchemy, the inner kind, which, if you allow it and aren't lazy in your inner work, can transform your life without any external chemicals, but purely through inner alchemy. Because the world is within us, and everything is within us.

❖ Research - Inner Work ❖

Study of Sacred Scriptures

I began to feel a strong urge to explore and understand sacred texts somewhere after the birth of my first child. This process has now lasted about ten years. The study of sacred books and writings, primarily from the Bible and the Gospels, as well as from every faith in this world and all the texts I could access, became my focus. At first, it was unreasonably difficult, but I was thirsty for truth and eager to learn everything. Many sleepless nights didn't weigh on me, despite family life and the responsibilities and struggles that life brings. My inner strength was stronger than ever before.

I started to decipher everything that came my way, constantly asking myself questions: "Okay, how can all this benefit humanity in the 21st century?" The Gospels of Matthew, Luke, John, and Mark, as well as the books of our biblical prophets and even those hidden from public view, speak volumes and open eyes and hearts when understood. These include the Gospels of Thomas, Mary Magdalene, and Philip. I did not stop at our sacred texts but moved on to the Torah, Hinduism, Buddhism, the Dhammapada, the Bhagavad Gita, the Tao Te Ching, as well as the teachings of Hermes Trismegistus and Kabbalah, and the complete Emerald Tablets of Egypt, which also include the writings of King Thoth.

To avoid listing everything, there are vast collections of such books. I did not read them literally; rather, I studied them, using them as material for exploration because I understood that all Divine souls used metaphors and parables to convey their messages through the ages, and that is a significant difference! Meanwhile, I spent every free moment in silence—what one might call meditation or prayer. However you interpret it, it is nothing more than being in silence.

Those who advocate for meditation as an enemy of the soul or the human being do not know the nature of God and divine aspects. Meditation is nothing more than being alone with oneself in silence, just as monks do. The play of names, when used, can be the most potent tool in the world, as we clearly see today. I was in such silences and depths. There were days when my silence lasted 4-5 hours, during which I received immense insights and revelations. Everything that interested me, I discovered with the help of that silence.

Today, as you may notice, the world is fighting against silence with technology that inundates us with unnecessary information, and if one doesn't take action, they remain trapped in a vicious cycle—or, as many call it, the matrix of life. But let's return to the story.

It's fortunate that I read everything, as one text provided answers to another. For instance, I found the words of Jesus in the book of King Thoth, which is 36,000 years old, while Jesus existed around 2,000 years ago. I realized that everything is encrypted, that everything is conveyed in parables, and little is known about Jesus's time in Egypt, where he received his teachings.

However, I won't delve into that direction right now. Essentially, my mind and soul began to connect the parables and codes, and everything started to align into one cohesive understanding. All the deciphering I struggled through during sleepless nights began to fit together like a grand puzzle of the soul and its journey. My mind was racing at 300 km/h, and all the energy centers in my body opened, from the smallest to the largest. That's when I realized that the seven angels mentioned in the Bible actually represent the seven chakras in Hinduism.

Moreover, the concept of the Trinity exists in almost all faiths, just presented differently. It's not about the external; rather, all these texts serve as signposts leading to the inner world—to realize that we are all

God's children. Just as Jesus told his apostles that they could do much more than he had done—there is truth in that.

In the following sections, I will provide and translate literally some of Jesus's sayings, and you will recognize them and understand their essence correctly. The literal meanings will be revealed to you, rather than the hidden and repackaged interpretations, as is often the case. Much has been altered or "lost," making it nearly impossible to access authentic texts. So, let's begin now with what is most important in all of this and the reason for my writing. Follow me.

❖ Jesus-The Kingdom of Heaven-Treasure for the Poor ❖

"BLESSED ARE THE POOR in spirit, for theirs is the kingdom of heaven."

Interpretation:

When you are light in spirit, when you shed all the burdens and guilt you carry from the past, your spirit becomes poor, and there is nothing weighing it down to the earth, or, as Buddhists would say, to the karmic wheel. In that moment, you are free from karma, and the feeling you carry is a sense of bliss within you—everything comes easily. This is achieved through silence—meditation. When Jesus healed people, he forgave them not because he was the Son of God, as we all are, but because every person has the power within themselves to forgive, primarily for their own sake. To forgive themselves for what they have done in the past or what has been done to them, which they have labeled as bad and given meaning to.

In the book *Tao Te Ching*, the similarity is reflected in the saying: "The nameless is the source of heaven and earth; the named is the mother of all things." From a young age, when things happen to us, we label them as good or bad, categorizing them within ourselves through the emotion we experience as good or bad.

However, we need to find the middle path that the great mystic Osho speaks about. Things are as they are—neither good nor bad in their essence, because everything comes from the same source, no matter how difficult that may be for us to understand at times.

When we are born, we are pure—pure consciousness, full of love and forgiveness. If you know a child or have your own, you know that a child does not hold onto anger; instead, it forgives in an instant and moves on, offering love and forgiveness. For a child, this is an instantaneous event. Here, I speak of a child before the age of seven, before it adopts a certain behavioral model from parents or the environment in which it grows up. Until the age of seven, a child is of pure consciousness, still connected to its soul, spiritual guide, or higher self.

It is essential to understand these words of Jesus, as well as all others, with their true meaning. Therefore, be light or poor in spirit, live, and recognize that experiences are simply what they are.

Through silence, begin to forgive and release everything from the past—forgive yourself and others, situations, events, people—everything that resides within you. Otherwise, these issues will continue to repeat in cycles in your life and won't pass until you overcome them. You will encounter similar circumstances and situations as in the past, experiencing the same emotions you've already felt, and you will wonder: Where is happiness?

It's like when a woman goes from one marriage to another, from one relationship to another, asking herself: Why do I keep running into fools, and why does everything repeat in cycles? This will persist until you master those lessons.

I am here to help you with that if you choose to follow the path rare traveled. I quote Osho again. Jesus understood everything and tried to convey it to people, but many, unfortunately, did not grasp the meaning of the words; they understood everything literally, and therein lies a great mistake that still prevents salvation among people today, with sorrow cutting like a sword.

"Love your enemies, bless those who curse you, do good to those who hate you, and pray for those who spitefully use you and persecute you."

Interpretation:

Jesus' words clearly speak of the inner path, not just the outer one. When Jesus speaks of enemies, he is actually referring to your other side – your other self. Every person carries within them both an angel and a devil, both Lucifer and Archangel Michael. All these forces reside within us, as the old story of "two wolves" says: "Beware of which wolf you feed."

"Love your enemies" means you must accept yourself, not selfishly or egotistically, but sincerely, with all those sides of you that separate you from Divine virtues. Love yourself as you are, with all your strengths and weaknesses. Acceptance of oneself is key because God wanted you exactly as you are. Before you came into this world, you defined your purpose and qualities.

Understand that God loves everyone – there is no one whom God does not love, and that is why you must reconcile with what you have done. Always keep in mind that everyone, including yourself, does their best in any given moment. It may look different from another perspective, but everyone acts according to what they know and can do at that time. If they knew better, they would do better. That is why God constantly says: "Rejoice, do not be afraid."

You are your own greatest enemy as long as you do not embrace and love your other side – the one that others do not see, which manifests when you are alone, behind closed doors. This "other side" can be understood as your inner child or your dark side.

But all of this is you. When Jesus says, "Bless those who curse you," he is speaking about those inner parts of yourself that do not give you peace – the negative thoughts you wish to avoid.

Bless those thoughts, release them, and you will see how, over time, you will become a master of this skill – the alchemist of your own life. Alchemy, in a spiritual sense, represents transformation – turning inner dark thoughts into golden ones, inner sadness into joy. When a negative thought arises, replace it with a positive one.

Engage in inner dialogues with yourself in silence until you achieve peace and become the master of your inner world. Pray for that within you that haunts you, forgive yourself for the past, because your mind cannot be truly happy if it is stuck in the past or the future. The power lies in the present moment, for God is always present here and now. Remember how God said to Moses in the desert: "I Am That I Am." This means that God is not the one who was or the one who will be, but the one who is – God is present now, in every present moment.

"AND NO ONE POURS NEW wine into old wineskins; otherwise, the new wine will burst the skins, and it will be spilled, and the wineskins will perish. But new wine must be put into new wineskins."

INTERPRETATION:

You cannot be the new you if you are still trying to pour new things into the old you and bring a new life to your old self. It's pointless to put masks of a new face on the old you because sooner or later you will "burst," and your anger, rage, and everything you hold inside unresolved will spill out. Cleanse yourself within; be poor in spirit (not in a material sense), and the spirit of truth will descend upon you, and you will be a new you – cleansed, enlightened, and liberated.

New wine (the new version of you) is to be poured into a new, purified you, and happiness will accompany you at every step.

What does Buddha tell us? "All that we are is the result of what we have thought: thoughts are everything. If a man speaks or acts with an evil thought, suffering follows him like the wheel follows the foot of the ox. If a man speaks or acts with a pure thought, happiness follows him like a shadow that never leaves."

So, be pure within yourself and pour new wine into yourself. Cleanse yourself of the past and do NOT JUDGE either yourself or others, for everything is as it is. Everything that happens to you is a result of what you have experienced but have not cleansed and reconciled within yourself. Because of this, it will always return to you in cycles until you master it, so to speak, until you reconcile with it – truly reconcile and move on. This is how karma is broken down and dissolved. This is how the path ahead of you is cleansed, and all cycles, one by one, will be overcome as you master them with inner peace. That's how they stop appearing in your physical world. For, "As within, so without."

Now, my dear ones, I hope this has become clearer to you. Do you notice how all of this is connected, how these parables and sayings are intertwined? How every faith in this world conveys a similar message in a different way—Jesus, Buddha, each for their own environment—some speak more clearly, others more cryptically, but "Whoever has ears, let them hear," right? Almost every time after finishing a parable, Jesus would say, "Whoever has ears, let them hear!" — and for a reason, of course, so that we might perceive and deeply understand everything he was trying to convey. How else could he have spoken for the message to be passed through centuries except in parables?

Let's be clear, these are teachings from a time when people didn't have concepts like consciousness and subconsciousness, so he might have said Father and Son instead? Adam and Eve? If you understand what I'm trying to tell you, when Jesus says, "I and the Father are one," replace those terms with consciousness and subconsciousness. In the Gospel of Philip, it says that Jesus and Christ are two names, more precisely, Jesus is a name, and Christ is a title after the crucifixion. Perhaps it's time for you to experience a crucifixion as well—but within you, an emotional crucifixion, because everything is within you.

There is much more you will discover in this and the next book. Truths will be presented to you that may shatter everything you thought was true, possibly even shake your belief system, but they will bring with them a treasure that no eye has seen nor ear heard—a treasure of an imperishable nature, now and forever. Follow me.

"So, if you bring your gift to the altar, and there remember that your brother has something against you, leave your gift there before the altar, and go; first be reconciled to your brother, then come and offer your gift."

Interpretation:

You know about the existence of your other self, that part of you which surfaces from time to time, especially when you least want it to. It's that person and those traits that come out, leaving you later saying to yourself: "Why did I react like that? Why did I let myself snap? Why did I say all those words? That wasn't me, I don't know what got into me!" Time passes, and a similar situation arises again, and once more, you snap—but it's not you, it's as if someone else is doing it. Sorry, but it's not some horned creature on your shoulder; that's all symbolism. It's not some entity with a pitchfork in hand that has special permission from God to do this to you. Again, from that same God who loves you unconditionally, but supposedly wants to test your patience and wear you down. And since He can't do it Himself, He'll create someone He allegedly can't destroy in the blink of an eye, and that someone will do the job, while God watches and decides if you are fit for the fire or for the light.

I will repeat once again here: God is ABSOLUTE LOVE, and you can experience that emotion only when you raise your consciousness high enough, which in Hinduism would be described as reaching the crown chakra. At that point, you become like God, or when you are touched by Archangel Michael, or when you find the Kingdom of Heaven that Jesus speaks of all the time. This is the highest level of human consciousness, which was possessed by the great superhuman Nikola Tesla and many others who have left their mark on this world, drawing inspiration for their work from the Divine Realm.

But let's get back to the topic. Your other self, which is destroying you, is your brother, and the altar is your mind and consciousness. That's why it's pointless to offer yourself gifts (positive thoughts and beliefs) if you have something against yourself or your other self that doesn't give you peace, subconsciously condemning you for the past—past events, people, and situations—or creating fear of tomorrow and the future. Make peace with your brother, with your other self within, which most often surfaces when we are in altered states of consciousness, for example, when we are too drunk or under the influence of substances that alter consciousness. As they say: "What a sober man thinks, a drunk man speaks."

Even that is a kind of guidance for consciousness.

So, the altar is your mind and your consciousness. When you make peace with your brother, meaning with yourself, then come and offer the gift of good thoughts and positive emotions before the altar, and it will be permanent because you will cleanse the internal blocks and obstacles that prevent you from having peace in your mind and soul.

Let me briefly touch on something. You have probably heard of the famous Law of Attraction, which is promoted and forms a kind of New Age religion, a religion of the new era. This operates on the principle that you can attract anything you want into your life if you think about it and visualize the image of the life you desire in your mind, and if you raise your vibration—meaning if your consciousness aligns with the scale where everything you desire exists—and, along with that, if you carry the emotional feeling as if your wish has already been fulfilled. I do not deny magnetism; like attracts like, and I do not deny that this can be achieved—I know it can, and there is great truth in it. My story about buying a car shows that.

But this is just one of the laws of the universe and God, and for it to work, your altar must be clean; your mind and soul must be free. Then ask for whatever you desire, and it will be given to you so that your happiness may be complete. We will talk more about all of this. What's important for you to know and remember is that your altar is your mind, and that inside of you is your brother, your other self. The sooner you reconcile with yourself, the sooner life will open up for you in unimaginable ways, and you will celebrate from the depths of your soul.

Jesus said, "Blessed is the lion that the man eats, and the lion will become man. Cursed is the man that the lion eats, and the lion will become man." (Gospel of Thomas)

INTERPRETATION:

SUCH A PARABLE FROM Jesus might seem overly confusing, and it took me a lot of time to decode. You'll see clearly if you replace the word "lion" with "ego" or with the animalistic part of our consciousness, which pulls us toward animal instincts. These are qualities in which we become slaves to habit, as animals are slaves to their instincts. When someone's ego is highly pronounced, it can be irritating to those around them and destructive to the person and their consciousness. Because the ego is just that—our other self, which prevents us from awakening all the divine aspects within us.

The ego can be constantly present, or it can manifest in certain situations. It can lead us to think we are more important than others. Let me be clear: we can be *special* in relation to others, and that's fine—being special means having more pronounced virtues or having a journey that is more unique than someone else's. But we are not more *important* because, to God, all people are the same. I would put it this way: the sun shines for the scholar and for the prisoner and for the monk. The same sun shines for everyone. Don't judge anyone's path because every path is different and unique.

Allow me to give an example: a man might judge a woman of "loose morals" who works on the street at night, and in some way, it may seem immoral to us that she earns a living that way. We may feel the urge to judge her, but her soul is the same soul that dwells within you—her path in this life is simply different. On a higher level, her soul has chosen certain experiences for this life. Do you think that by judging her, you will become more important than she is? I wouldn't say that. Your "leash" in this life is much shorter. If God were to loosen the leash on you—symbolically speaking, of course—and let it be as long as hers, how much would you be able to endure? Could you bear it?

Life has taught me that by judging others, we can very easily end up in their situations. That's why the ego must fall or be reduced to a minimum.

If the ego falls, the love for the world and everything around you will explode within you like an atomic bomb, and you will become pure love. If you reduce the ego to a minimum, you will destroy the blockages in your consciousness, and the river of good energy and prosperity will flow through you and your life without obstacles. Understand in essence and realize that God is a single whole that has divided into a million parts, but each part is a part of God. Every part forms one God. It is like how a wave in the ocean is part of the sea—the wave is just an expression of the ocean, but it is not land; it belongs to the sea.

Whether bigger or smaller, the wave is a part of the ocean. In the same way, God, the creator of everything, dwells within everything. When you understand this with both your mind and soul, joy will shine within you because you will know that you are not separated from anything or anyone, especially not from the Creator. He is you, and you are Him, or He is a part of you, and you are a part of Him.

God created people, and people collectively create and make up God. It's a reciprocal process. The ego, when overly expressed, makes us feel separated from things and pushes us to judge something or someone, not knowing that we are, in essence, judging God and His creation, as well as ourselves, when we judge others. This is the illusion of separation. But, of course, without the illusion of separation, there would be no need for collapsing it and reuniting with God. When you leave this place, you will instantly know everything. That is why Jesus speaks of the importance of resurrection while alive—because it is here, in this life, that we created the problem, here we became separated, and it is here that we must reunite.

This brings about the absolute reunion with the Creator of everything, who is not a man with a beard but permeates our entire existence in the form of energy and consciousness.

God dwells within us, and we dwell in God. Therefore, we must strive to minimize the ego and avoid judging others' lives and their paths. What matters to us is our own path and how we can bring our existence closer to God—understanding that we are all one on the same journey. We should run together toward the goal, not race to see who gets there first.

The highest goal is the same for everyone, and that is to raise our consciousness above animalistic instincts and ways of thinking, and to see the bigger picture. When consciousness is elevated enough, trust me, the feelings that will carry you will be unlike anything you've ever experienced before, known only to a select few people in the world.

"If your leaders say to you, 'The Kingdom of Heaven is in the sky,' then the birds of the sky will precede you. If they say, 'It is in the sea,' then the fish will precede you. But the Kingdom is actually within you and around you, and you do not see it. When you come to know yourselves, you will realize that you are the sons of the living Father. But if you do not come to know yourselves, you will live in poverty, and you yourselves will be that poverty." (Gospel of Thomas)

<hr>

INTERPRETATION:

It is clear what this is about—sharply and plainly stated, if only we want to fully understand and accept these words of Jesus. Everything is within you and around you. It's in vain if your senses delight in stories or in the comfort that the Kingdom is somewhere out there, that only when you leave this life will everything be as it should. We are all waiting for something—better times to be better ourselves, situations to change so we can become better. We wait for this, we wait for that, yet we do not react to such statements made by the greatest Divine souls.

There are beliefs so deeply embedded in us that they serve no purpose after thousands of years, yet we still live by them because, well, it's easier that way. And it's a great excuse to delay everything we are capable of doing, and we are capable of so much—if only we start, if we begin working on our inner self, on our inner world.

If it's easier for someone to ignore this, then perhaps this is not for them. This is for those souls hungry for answers and words that mean something, words that literally convey the meanings of people who lived on Earth, who realized the truth, inspired by light, and wished for others to know it too.

For Jesus also says, "You are the light of the world. A city set on a hill cannot be hidden. Neither do people light a lamp and put it under a bowl. Instead, they put it on its stand, and it gives light to everyone in the house. In the same way, let your light shine before others, that they may see your good deeds and glorify your Father in heaven."

I am writing all of this for that very reason—so it may remain for those who have those ears, the inner ear, to hear and understand this, because light spreads further. I long for justice, to share it with you, to lift the veils from your eyes. Whoever is meant to receive this message will hear it, understand it, and attempt to apply all of these teachings.

Where is the Kingdom of Heaven within you? I will explain this to you specifically in the next interpretation, delving deeper into what you need to realize: that the Kingdom is within you, that you possess an immense power inside of you, waiting to be awakened and revealed by applying the principles I am writing about in this book. Don't let anyone deceive or mislead you anymore. Take one or two steps, and the rest will flow from you like a river. When you see how this book helps you break the chains of beliefs that, for all these years, have not helped—not just you, but anyone—be wiser and smarter.

That's where Jesus' words come in: "Be wise as serpents and harmless as doves." Work on yourself in silence, be calm, forgive, and cast away all the judgments you hold against yourself from your soul. What has been, is past; what will be is uncertain and depends solely on you. You have free will, don't you? Free to either leave it to the aspect of fate (the cycles of life) to carry you along or to use the power you possess to transform yourself. In either case, life will flow. If you begin to cleanse the past, you are at the same moment changing the future, for you are clearing that path

Know that everything is in cycles and everything repeats itself. Some cycles happen on an annual basis, some are a bit stronger and occur every 3 years, some every 7 years, some every 12 years, but everything moves, and nothing remains still. Cycles come; perhaps the circumstances and people change, but the emotional feelings that repeat themselves follow the same pattern, and they come from that. Once you cleanse everything, there will be no more cycles. You will be like a child—if you are familiar with that saying of Jesus that "children inherit the Kingdom of Heaven"—and forgive not just 7 times, but 77 times if necessary, not for the sake of others, but for your own sake. Submerge the ego in those situations and forgive solely for yourself, because that other person is you. God is within us all.

Once, a good friend of mine, Mijo, who is no longer with us but was a profound soul, said to me: "I wrote in a journal for years, but when I realized that everything was repeating, that I was writing the same and similar things again, at one point I fearfully threw the journal away, and since then, I haven't written anymore." And he was right. He recognized the repeating cycles in life. Now, I will explain to you the place of the Kingdom of Heaven within you in the next interpretation.

————— ◈ —————

"DO NOT WORRY, THEN, saying: What will we eat, or what will we drink, or with what will we be clothed? But seek first the Kingdom of Heaven and its righteousness, and all these things will be added to you."

————— ◈ —————

INTERPRETATION:

The best testimony for this is the first part of the book, where I describe my life and its obstacles. I am not more important, but I have had a special journey. I believe that, unfortunately, many people have this. This is all for you, my dear ones. Seek ways to overcome what is within you, for we know that the Kingdom is within us, and I am providing you with some methods to reach the Kingdom through all these deciphered parables. Do not worry about earthly things, for you are more valuable than that. You will always have enough to move from one moment to the next. No matter how unreal it may sometimes seem, you have always had enough, even to come to this book and read it. Remember what you have been through in life, and here you are, reading this book, and it will remain so forever. My parents waited for better times, and their parents waited for better times, and political changes, and economic changes, and all possible changes in worry, in fear. But look at what is written in this parable: do not worry; you will always have enough. Here, I am not talking about desires, those things we might want on a physical level; perhaps, at that moment, due to our predetermined path, it does not align on a soul level, and we burn with unfulfilled desires and enter into judgments: "How does he have this, and I do not?" and "He has challenges." Do not worry about that; we all have them; the roles are just currently such. But everything will be added to you if you seek the Kingdom of Heaven first.

I have had a million such adversities in my life. Sometimes friends carried me on their backs so that I and my family could survive. But I do not forget; I also carry friends on my back when needed, and those I do not know. I always give what I can of myself in every sense. The greatest foolishness is that we wait for God while rejecting people. But God works through people, or we expect Him to descend personally to drop money into our pockets and provide everything else we want and need.

Praying to God for our desires is like trying to teach God how to do His job. He already knows what we need even before we think of it; do not worry about that. As I write this, I am trying to find the right words so that you understand what I want to say about the Kingdom. The Kingdom of Heaven is the most beautiful and sublime feeling a person can experience, and then they are one with God, one with their Creator. Perhaps I would put it this way: when you cleanse your past, which you carry like weights on your back, when you eliminate self-judgment and arrogance toward others, and drown that ego, the very gates of paradise will open for you. While you are alive, you will experience the Kingdom of Heaven within you. You will be full of joy, knowing that you are reborn. There will be no more dark side within you, only the beauty of life. Everything flows, and everything goes smoothly. Problems may start to knock you down, or rather, challenges may arise, but they cannot bring you down. You are pure, new, and humble in spirit, light as a feather. You simply flow through life, as Buddha speaks of it. Just as the Tao Te Ching says, Tao is the river, the flow of life. The Tao that cannot be named is the eternal Tao.

So what does this mean? We mentioned the naming of things above, and God is the eternal Tao. The Kingdom of Heaven is the eternal Tao. In Indian faith or Hinduism, it is believed that a person has seven energy centers. In Christianity, we have seven archangels, headed by Archangel Michael. They are: Gabriel, Raphael, Uriel, Sealtiel, Jefrem, Barahiel.

And the seven chakras go from the lowest to the highest: Muladhara (Root Chakra), Svadhisthana (Sacral Chakra), Manipura (Solar Plexus), Anahata (Heart Chakra), Vishuddha (Throat Chakra), Ajna (Third Eye Chakra), Sahasrara (Crown Chakra). The last or crown chakra is located at the top of the head. When you become poor in spirit, the flow of energy within you flows like a river, and your energy reaches the crown chakra. At that point, you attain a state of consciousness called nirvana or the Kingdom of Heaven as described by Jesus. Your altar is then pure, and gifts will simply come.

If Jesus had said this in another way, when the spectrum of words like energy, frequency, and vibration, which Nikola Tesla speaks about, was available 2,000 years ago, he might have said: "Do not worry about what you will eat or drink. Just seek a way to elevate your energy to the highest level of consciousness, and all else will be added to you." And here you use the truth of sincerity towards yourself, not fog and illusions, because Jesus said: 'I am the way, the truth, and the life.' For then you overcome all karmic cycles and obstacles, as all of that exists at a lower level, and you rise above it.

Now imagine that murderer or a person in deep depression—at what level of energy are they? Would they be the same or do the same if they were at the highest level or at least close to the peak of that consciousness? I would say no, because there resides absolute love for people, sincere, unforced, and untainted. And what is absolute love? It is when I love you simply because you are, not because of what you do, bring, or take away. Not just because of your virtues, but because I know you, I know your soul, who you are, where you come from. I don't see you as competition in life; I love you simply because you exist. That can only come from God or a person who reaches Divine consciousness.

And yes, all will be added to you. You will attract everything at that level of consciousness, which is abundance of all kinds. You will be in happiness without exception! Ah, that Kingdom of Heaven may seem unreal, but once you experience it, it is the finest taste, the most beautiful scent, the best sound, the softest touch. That is God. Is it worth it to strive for that, to take all the steps to reach it, to dedicate time to your inner work when the reward is unimaginable? That is what we all strive for, but we are directed toward everything contrary to that. Again, Nikola Tesla said, "If you want to find the secrets of the universe, think in terms of energy, frequency, and vibration." There it is, the trinity at work!

Through righteousness, one arrives at this state, and that is the feeling of equality towards everything, towards people who are and are not your close relatives, towards everyone. This doesn't mean you should give everything to everyone and trample on yourself. On the contrary, it means carrying those feelings with you everywhere, living with those emotions and feelings. You don't have to help, but don't hinder either. Mercy, both physical and spiritual, are two separate things, yet they form a whole.

You must apply spiritual mercy to yourself, be merciful towards yourself, and understand that everything outside this present moment, everything that has happened, is not worth mentioning. There's a reason the windshield of a car is large while the rearview mirrors are small. You look at them only to orient yourself, while you look ahead to see clearly where you are going. Don't reverse this.

I hope I have managed to explain this sufficiently for now. I would like to move on to that famous parable in which Jesus speaks about slapping and turning the other cheek, which will clarify something you may not even suspect when you turn inward instead of just focusing on external events.

Jesus said: "But I say to you, do not resist an evil; but whoever slaps you on your right cheek, turn the other to him also."

INTERPRETATION:

WHAT WILL HAPPEN IF a person approaches you on the street and slaps you across the right cheek? And you turn the other cheek; he will probably hit you again. Once he sees he can do that, he will start hitting and punching you in the face and body. When he knocks you to the ground, he might stop there, if he has even a little mercy in him, and walk away in pride, while you lie on the ground in pain, likely bleeding, waiting for emergency assistance. But you know what? God will judge him, and you might manage to get up, straighten yourself, with a ton of painkillers, hide, and run away so you don't encounter him again, because he will see that he can repeat this at some point. And all this just so you can gain some label of martyrdom, in the sense that when you leave this world, you go straight to heaven! A direct line, VIP section!

Forgive my irony here; far from preferring violence, but let's be realistic: a person must defend themselves or someone who needs it; otherwise, where is the justice? Or will you approach someone who has been beaten up and say, "Hey, don't worry, there's a special place waiting for you in heaven for this; the doctors will come soon, so take it easy." Again, I'm being ironic, I know, but the falsehood and injustice hurt me deeply. Let's get to the point. I told you that everything happens in cycles. Until we master them, when we do, they won't repeat, and with fighting against cycles, we will not succeed; instead, we begin to work on forgiveness and letting go. As you read this book, you may find yourself in some cycle in life, and let's be clear: just as there are negative cycles, there are also positive ones. Thank God for that! It is clearly stated here: when a negative cycle comes, when we are expected to react violently, to explode and go crazy inside, we should remain calm, composed, and peaceful. So when we get hit, let it hit; here's the other cheek. I do not resist because I know I will overcome that negativity. Only by reacting differently.

Can fear heal fear? The same energy cannot overcome the same energy. Now, imagine: a cycle is coming, a negative period, because what is buried within you as fear, pain, anger, and sadness is manifesting and showing itself in the physical world before you.

And this cycle is coming, and you are energetically elevated, raising your consciousness almost to that heavenly kingdom or the crown chakra. You are victorious even before the cycle reaches you because you have primarily conquered yourself, as you have cleansed that part of yourself. And the lesson for your soul is unnecessary; it is meaningless if it has been mastered and serves no purpose in your life. You may always have challenges from those close to you and people you care about, as they must strive for it just as you do. Jesus told us: "Everyone bears their own cross." I can help you a lot and guide you so that you no longer wander, but you must carry your own cross, just as I must carry mine.

Will you carry it or leave it behind, knowing you will have to bear it sooner or later? That is already up to you: whether you will begin your inner work on yourself or not. That is already your choice, isn't it? That's why it is completely right and the only important thing to turn the other cheek. In that case, the only effective response is to bless those who persecute you and move on. I willingly turn the other cheek here; I surrender immediately because surrender is victory. I won't give it any significance, and it will diminish and disappear because it is unnecessary. There is nothing more to learn from it, and a part of the shackles has fallen to the ground. The soul is freer and lighter and is on the path to liberation.

Some things will go smoothly, while others will require more effort, but if you stay on the path, you will eventually triumph. And the reward is not short-lived and perishable, like what we receive our whole lives, but something eternal and lasting, and it is important that it happens while one is alive. Something that matters for both this world and the next, toward which we are heading and getting closer. And whether we will start all over again is up to us and our free will.

"And when you pray, go into your room, and when you have shut your door, pray to your Father who is in secret; and your Father who sees in secret will reward you openly."

INTERPRETATION:

These words are not that difficult to understand, and when you take yourself as a starting point, they gain even more meaning. "Your room" can be interpreted as "your own space." You may not know this or have noticed it, but Jesus always prayed alone. Whatever he was doing during the day and whoever he was with, he always separated himself from the apostles when he wanted to pray. He always prayed—meditated—alone, in his unique relationship with his inner self, with his Father, with his subconscious. Take yourself, your inner being, your interior as "your room," and you will understand.

Enter into "your room," into yourself, close your eyes in silence, relax your mind and body, and shut the door to the outside world, for the whole world is hidden within you. Explore it. Resolve conflicts with yourself there, have dialogues with your dark side there, reconcile with your brother in "your room," in your altar, in your inner space.

Scientists now explain through research and measurements of the human mind that our mind has different states of operation, so to speak, and to simplify: starting from a state of high mental activity called gamma waves, then the state of alertness – beta waves, followed by alpha waves as a state of relaxed awareness, gentle meditation or drowsiness, then theta waves – the state of deep meditation, dreaming, or REM phase that leads us into dreams, and the deepest state – delta waves – deep sleep without dreams, the body's regeneration.

When you spend 4-5 hours in a meditative state, as I have, like monks with their immense skills in calming the body, the experiences you go through are fascinating. You gain insights and answers and connect with the divine aspects of consciousness that are unknown to many, yet everyone carries them within themselves. Here resides God; this is where the deepest part of consciousness dwells—your second self, which knows and understands everything. You don't have to enter such states; it is enough to go within, into "your room," relax in silence, and let your thoughts flow. Believe me, they will come like on a conveyor belt.

Here, you will use the keys to calming down, which I will elaborate on in the upcoming books, and simply breathe. You breathe deeply and relax. Do not identify with your thoughts, for those thoughts are not you. The brain is always active, working 24 hours a day, and it does not stop even when you sleep. In the universe, nothing is truly still; even when you sit or lie down, you are doing something.

Within you, trillions of cells operate at an incredible speed, keeping your body alive and active. Thus, the content of our life experiences is found and flows through our thoughts. This is why I insist so much on inner work because that silence calms your mental waves, and as it calms them, it expands your awareness of the world and of what you carry within you. And when you recognize what surfaces in that silence, you will know what needs to be addressed. While it is buried, it remains hidden and secret, operating in the subconscious, and manifests in the physical world before you.

Let's immediately move on to what Jesus says about what is hidden within you and how it affects your life and the world you live in.

"If you bring forth what is within you, what you have will save you. If you do not have it within you, what you do not have will destroy you." (Gospel of Thomas)

INTERPRETATION:

Here we are! This is what we seek and use; this is why we swim and run into silence, like small children running towards their parents. Here are our roots of existence, here is our first thought, our first conflict with ourselves, our neglected inner child, our second "self," filled with all the traumas of sadness and pain, the unresolved and unhealed situations that are packed within us like a storage unit, and which manifest in cycles before us in the physical world. We feel like we are in the whirlwind of life, like on a roller coaster; emotions operate on a scale from deep sadness to high happiness, then back to pain and sorrow, up towards joy, then down to fear. Just when we take steps forward, there comes a cycle in the form of a lesson, and we stumble and fall. A period comes when we think we can do anything (which is true), but then a situation arises again, and in the blink of an eye, we are down—mentally, emotionally, physically, psychologically exhausted—and the question follows: "God, why?"

At this level of bodily thinking, we do not know why. If we reach out for external help, there are the calming pills because we cannot consciously live with ourselves, and we do not know where all this comes from. I do not blame or judge anything, dear ones, because we do not know what or who we are fighting at that moment, and the struggle is internal!

When I have a problem with you, I can sit down at a table with you, and we will smooth things over and resolve misunderstandings with words. But when I have a problem with something within myself, whom do I sit with? Who do I point my finger at? That is when you go into silence, where you sit at the table with yourself—your brother, sister, mother, wife, etc. No matter how you see and name your other side, you then engage in dialogue and resolve it through love, forgiveness, and blessing for that other side of you. There is no judgment or blame, only forgiveness and release, for that other side is you and a part of you. So embrace and love it.

The expression of inner sadness and pain is trying to tell you something you need to work on, but you suppress and ignore it, and it becomes angry at you, while you become angry at yourself and everything around you. Then you attract into your life everything contrary to what you desire. You know what? Sometimes you might stumble upon something good, a bit of happiness for a while, but your other side is constantly calling you for reconciliation. So, reconcile with it!

Everything else external only leads to even greater pressure, or rather, to the suppression of what lies deep within us and seeks a way to be expressed and treated. There are very few methods that I acknowledge externally.

One of them is that sometimes, for certain things, it's enough to have a deep conversation with the right person to feel relief. This will help to ease the tension in the nerves and allow a person to unload through the expression of emotions. And then, I urge you, hurry into silence! The kind I've been talking about all along.

Some external methods are not only ineffective but can also lead you to destructive beliefs, words like: "We are guilty, born and created in the sin of our ancestors, the washing machine on the holy day..." I apologize, but there is nothing holier than you, for every day is holy in which your consciousness has become sacred. Sometimes certain stories remind me of Hansel and Gretel and offend my spirit and intelligence. May I tell you? You were not born in sin! You were not created by some mistake of God, for God does not make mistakes.

Did God know that Eve would eat the apple? If He didn't, then He isn't God, because God is the incomprehensible absolute, the creator of everything; He is in everything and permeates all existence. In short—He knows everything. If He did know that Eve would eat the apple, it means He consciously allowed it to happen in order to cast them out of the Garden of Eden, and since then, for thousands of years, He waits above to send you to eternal hellfire every day. He has a beard and looks down at Earth with a frown, shouting: "Aha, I'm just watching you!" Does God need this drama, or is He bored and just having a little fun? Please, wake up! It's time to awaken!

There is a factor of faith that is very strong because Jesus said, "According to your faith, let it be done to you!" If I present you with a story about a washing machine, and you deeply adopt the belief that something will happen if you just think about turning it on, then believe me, it will very easily happen or not—according to your faith, let it be done to you! How you believe is how it will ultimately be for you. This applies to all other beliefs we have adopted that have imprisoned our souls. And why according to your faith? Because you have unseen powers within you; you just keep them locked away and closed.

You are not to blame; that's how we've been taught from birth—not only in our region but very few religions almost none talk about the power of man and these things. It's easier for everyone to be in fear and adopt already pre-programmed beliefs, simply conforming to the need for something external, and we need an external scapegoat for our difficulties and life challenges—this one horned creature that commands an army directed against you, and everything is against you, and life is against you, while God watches and indifferently waits to see where He will place you. What a lovely compromise! But God is not there; you won't find Him there.

What you carry and have within you will either save you or destroy you. When you go inside yourself, you will see what you have within— all those unresolved conflicts and traumas. Through forgiveness, as many times as it takes—7 or 77 or 777—until you let them go, do it, repeat it, release it, bless it, reconcile with it, and it will save you. On the contrary, if you do not bring it out, it will manifest externally in cycles, weaken you, take your life energy, and ultimately destroy you. My dear, as you read this, know that you are loved! Please, never forget that! Please understand that you are a powerful being, the apple of God's eye, that you are His reflection. Please, never give up on yourself! You are not born and conceived in any sin, but from the union of the two most beautiful divine energies—masculine and feminine—and the holiest expression of love from your parents, who are also God's children. God is yours, and you are His; we are all one. Awaken the love in your heart because Jesus represents love; Jesus is love.

Forgive everyone and everything! They don't even have to know that you did it; go within yourself and forgive—for yourself and for your own sake. You don't have to ring all the bells to announce that you have forgiven; cleanse yourself internally, for that is what saves. Purify your spirit, make it light and simple, and you will see everything; you will see again, heavenly soul. I am just reminding you—you already know all this.

You already have all of this within you, because you are not here for the first time; you have lived, dear soul, you live, and you will live forever, and after death, you will not taste death. This is God's and Jesus's promise, but you must rise while you are alive. "Die before you die" — that is the key. I can explain and decipher every record, every parable for you. Follow my work and work on yourself, because I, my dear, have gone through that as well.

Do you see what my life has been like? And that is just a fraction — 34 years, which I have now, cannot fit into all the pages; it is just a fragment. I want to reveal to you the greatest secret of all at the end of this book.

It is about the personality I mention in this book — the Divine Consciousness, Jesus Christ.

Truly, truly I say to you: whoever believes in me will do the works that I do; and greater works than these will he do; and whatever you ask in my name, that I will do, that the Father may be glorified in the Son.

INTERPRETATION:

Jesus speaks "with faith in love," because Jesus represents and is that part of our consciousness that is pure love. We can create or do the same things he did, even greater works than his. Love today is not highly valued; we are energetically blocked in that part of our consciousness, which is understandable when we realize how lost we have become in some illusions of this world. But if it were valued, who would do anything wrong to anyone? When we act from love, it is always for the benefit of ourselves or the people we meet in our lives.

When Jesus says, "Ask in my name," how can this be interpreted? It can be interpreted however you want, but I know how it should be. We are not speaking literally in the name of Jesus, saying: "I ask for this and that in the name of Jesus," because that is too obvious. You know that there are countless unanswered prayers. People pray and pray, yet things remain unresolved and desires unfulfilled. Is the problem in the words we speak? Do we need to correct our words? Should we hum our prayers or hit a special tone for the desire we want? Of course not – nothing needs to change except ourselves. Everything else, when you change your inner self, will change externally.

To understand this well, let's see what Jesus represents. Who is Jesus? What is he like? What qualities does he possess? Jesus is our divine aspect, a reflection of perfection, and above all, a reflection of fully elevated consciousness, filled with love for humanity. If you notice, even in films about Jesus, you see that sometimes he can be quite bold with the Pharisees, loudly reprimanding some people around him, and he can become annoyed when they listen to him but do not understand the message he is conveying. You know that he entered the temple and began to overturn everything.

In this event, Jesus arrives in Jerusalem and enters the temple. In protest against the commercialization of the temple, Jesus begins overturning tables and causing disruption. So, He exhibits human qualities, just like you and me, and all of us, right? If anyone disputes this, they are disputing the Gospels in the New Testament according to Matthew, Mark, Luke, and John. These are His human traits, and that's normal because He is constantly trying to explain something to the people that is meant to save them, but they take it lightly and don't listen. He could have easily kept all the knowledge to Himself and conquered everything there is to conquer, but He didn't.

I emphasize, a lamp is not kept hidden; the light of the lamp is shared with the world, which is why this book exists right now. I talked about this in the previous texts. He is driven by justice because He possesses knowledge that He selflessly shares, and people fail to acknowledge it.

Jesus is an enlightened figure, pure energy, the pure Tao (river) of life, who was tested in the desert until He conquered His inner demons. And we see this outwardly in the form of the snake and Jesus in the desert. When He achieved fully elevated consciousness, He hurried back to the world to proclaim the path to inner purity. Did He forgive? Yes, He did. And He endured the most difficult things in the world—whipping, nails in His hands and feet, rejection, humiliation, the crown of thorns on His head—and in the midst of the greatest humiliation and unimaginable physical pain, He said: "Forgive them, Father, for they do not know what they are doing." Now, tell me, what is it that you cannot forgive? You, me, all of us? What is it in your life that we, these significant people, cannot forgive? This is so important for us and everything this book talks about, that if you were to just reflect a little, you would see the fruits that forgiveness brings.

Jesus is forgiveness, Jesus is faith, Jesus is love. If you are seeking something in your life, and you have forgiven yourself and others for everything, and you are seeking it through love as an emotion, if you are asking for it out of love for your benefit and for the benefit of others, and you have faith that you have already received it, know that it will come to you. It is inevitable, it is not a possibility or an option, it is certain.

"Ask of the Father in my name"—this means in the name of who He is and what He represents—and the Father will be glorified through His son. You will receive what you desire, whatever it may be. But open your heart to it. See it in your mind as already resolved for you. Ask for everything in the name of love and goodwill. Imagine how what you receive can be shared with those around you, for the Father will then touch your life and give you what you ask for, and you will continue to share it with others. Starting today, touch someone else's life. Every act of giving is an act of goodness, not just monetary. Give a smile to people, give empathy, offer comforting words, give love. Spread love—the only important thing in life—because God loves you, no matter who you are. There is no one whom God does not love. A person may get lost, hurt, or cause pain, but God is always waiting to embrace His child again and guide them.

At the level of the body, many things can happen—mistakes can be made, and one can act improperly—but at the level of your soul, you are God's. The soul, like the most high form, comes into this world and says, "I am going to experience certain things, but I know who I am at every moment." Then it is born into the physical world, takes a bodily form, and gets intoxicated and lost in this world, carried away by false beliefs. It lives and one day departs, saying, "I can't believe I got drunk, I'm going back again, this time I won't forget." And so it returns, intoxicated once more. But one day it will sober up. Why not now? When, if not now? Here are the keys, I am giving them to you right now, my dear ones.

Remind yourselves, and remember. Just place the key in the lock and turn it. Walk through that door. I am here beside the door, but you must walk through your own door, just as I have through mine. Do not be afraid, and rejoice, for the truth is right in front of you.

Jesus said: "I stood in the midst of the world, and I appeared to them in the flesh. I found them all drunk, and I did not find any among them thirsty. And my soul was sorrowful for the sons of men, for they are blind in their hearts, and do not see that they have come into the world empty, and they seek to leave it empty. But now they are drunk. When they sober up, they will repent."

"Drunk" in this context means spiritually unconscious, misled, unaware. The thirst that Jesus speaks of, which he did not find, refers to the fact that no one seeks true knowledge. Instead, everyone accepts what is served to them without question. They do not examine the faces of heaven and earth, nor do they examine themselves.

And He grieved for the sons of men because such great power is left untapped, while we struggle within our own thoughts and get lost, intoxicated by ego and greed. We use some kind of defense mechanism against everything that isn't of our own blood, yet the same blood flows through all of us. When they sober up, they will repent. Life is in no hurry; God is an endless process of creation—building and tearing down, there is always time. If you don't make it in this lifetime, there is time in other lifetimes.

Indians believe in reincarnation, and from my perspective, I have seen that it is indeed a truth. But people there also think, "There is time, we are born and we die, if not in this life, then in the next." Yet the soul has an incredible need to free itself as quickly as possible from the chains that will grant it freedom in both this life and after this life. That is why you must not be either drunk or blind. Open your heart, and whatever you seek, seek it through love.

But this seeking cannot be done with words; it must be done with emotion. When you feel in your heart what you seek and persevere in that feeling, you must feel it within yourself—love, the emotion of love—and act through it. I hope that we have explained here, in great detail, what it means to seek in the name of Jesus.

Jesus said, "When you make the two into one, and when the inner becomes as the outer, and the outer as the inner, and the upper as the lower, and when you make the male and the female into one, so that the male will no longer be male, and the female no longer female, then you will enter the Kingdom."

INTERPRETATION:

What a beautiful and wisely crafted parable or riddle! It's no wonder that Jesus' teachings have endured through the ages. This is probably the most challenging metaphor, one that was almost impossible for me to grasp at first. What are the two that need to be made into one? The inner? The outer? Male no longer being male, and female no longer being female?

For some of Jesus' metaphors, it took me months of working on just one, and believe me, I have deciphered them all—not just Jesus, but all sacred writings. Alongside exhausting mental effort, it required deep silence in which I dwelled to understand them, because the most important conversations happen in the silence ofthe mind. But it was worth it, because this is life, theseare the keys to the world, this is the essence of everything.

Let me explain, dear ones, when you make the two into one... Wow, how deep this metaphor is! But Jesus always knew what He was talking about, and so it is here as well. When you reconcile with yourself, when you unite within yourself both energies—you may call them masculine and feminine, angel and devil, or that brother you need to visit before offering your gift at the altar. It is that inner reconciliation within you that must happen.

To accept yourself, to forgive yourself (I keep repeating this), to forgive others through yourself and within yourself. To bring yourself back to peace and reconcile with yourself, to look in the mirror and say, "Hey, you've been through so much and survived it all, good for you, well done!" To look at yourself and say, "Thank you, and I love you." When was the last time you patted yourself on the back and said, "Well done for everything I've been through, and here I am, standing and moving forward!"

The idea that loving yourself is selfish is pure nonsense. If you don't love yourself, how will you love others? I'm not talking about narcissistic, ego-driven love—the "me, me, me" type. I'm talking about loving your existence, loving the fact that you are here. There are many souls who were never created, but you were created, you exist. God wanted you here, God wanted you to exist. Surely, something would be missing from existence if you weren't here, or do you think that God is an incompetent creator who works randomly without knowing what He's doing? Maybe some people don't know what they're doing, but God knows exactly what He's doing. When I talk about God, I'm talking about the Creator. Do you understand the depth of God? I mean the Creator of everything that exists—on every level: spiritual, material, and soulful. To create a human being, to create planets, the infinite universe, the earth, water, fire, the heavens—that is the God I'm talking about, not a limited concept in our minds. And He is within you right now, always within you and all around you.

When Jesus says, "Let the male no longer be male, and the female no longer be female," speaking of the inner and outer, the upper and lower, He is referring to division, because this world is one of polarities: up-down, left-right, hot-cold, positive-negative—everything has its opposite. When you unite all of these into one, then the spirit of energy, which is pure treasure, will be poured out upon you, and you will flourish in every sense. Through you will flow an inexhaustible inspiration, which you can direct and transform into any sphere of your life.

If you have forgotten, this book is written by someone who was separated from formal education, someone who can be socially deemed "incompetent." Due to school grades for some educational purposes. Someone who is encountering writing and expression for the first time.

Inspiration is complete and comes from within, and without modesty, you can become one of the most significant people on Earth if you channel it accordingly. Most people who have influenced humanity were divinely inspired, having entered the Kingdom, where no boundaries exist. In that state of consciousness, there are no limits.

I cannot explain to you enough what that feels like—it must be felt and experienced. "Ask, and it will be given to you; knock, and it will be opened to you." Reach that state I mentioned earlier. Things are what they are, and everything is as it is. From point A to point B, you have always had enough, made it through, and healed. But whether you worried or believed in the meantime—that is up to you. It's your free will.

Your Heavenly Father knows your physical needs. Don't worry, and don't absorb all sorts of stories from TV screens or internet portals—especially while you're working on this, until you solidify yourself. Because, believe me, you don't know what you are dealing with. I'm not condemning these things—it's always up to us what we choose to consume, both physically and spiritually. Just keep working on yourself. In a way, the world is upgrading itself as it knows how, and as God allows.

Here is my life story—let it serve as an example that destruction of unimaginable magnitude can bring prosperity. Do you think about that while the destruction is happening? Of course not, and it's incredibly difficult and painful, but in the end, it carries a profound message and deep transformation—both on a personal level and on a collective level of consciousness. You can handle destruction more easily only if you understand its purpose. And for that, a highly elevated awareness is necessary.

My dear ones, we are drawing this to a close. This is enough for the first book, enough for your mind, enough for your soul as a starting point. This is a process of information that your mind and soul need to process. Give them time, and if necessary, return to certain parts of this book. Or simply read through it until you absorb it, and share the light with the people around you. You might touch someone and help them greatly on their life path. My good souls, we are all one. I love you.

In future books or in certain seminars, I will talk about karma and continue to guide you toward deeper things, not in a complicated or enigmatic way, but directly and clearly so that it's understandable. I will speak about what karma is, but not the commercialized version, not the one the world has modernized to be seen as some instant consequence. Karma is movement, action, and a lesson to be mastered. I want to bring you and myself home, to return us to ourselves—that is what my life, my path, and my truth are all about. But we will continue these conversations, whether live or through writings, in the future.

❖ SOMETHING TO PONDER ❖

"The Pharisees and the scribes took the keys of knowledge and hid them. They did not enter, nor did they allow those who wanted to enter. But you be wise as serpents and innocent as doves."

❖ FINAL WORD ❖

Dear readers,

This book represents only a small part of my journey, filled with losses, struggles, and difficult moments I've gone through, but also awakenings, the discovery of inner strength, and understanding of sacred texts. Personally, I would have loved to have had such explanations and insights on my path because instead of a mountain of books read and interpretations made, I would have had everything at my fingertips; it would have been up to me to use and apply it. But I chose the road less traveled, a path that required much time, effort, and dedication—many headaches in contemplation and interpretation, then applying and testing every point because everything I write is what I have tried, experientially confirmed, and lived. I am still traveling this path, which requires much mental work and, of course, a lot of silence. But believe me, this has always been the goal: to help myself and then share selflessly so that your soul may rejoice just as mine does. As you have read, my desire has been to convey knowledge that you can apply in everyday life through the deciphering of just some of Jesus' words and messages he left us.

Self-discovery is a journey, not a destination. Through it, we uncover the essence of existence, overcome pain, trauma, and suffering, and rediscover the light that guides us.

Jesus' words, which have been interpreted in various ways for centuries, hold profound strength, but their true power lies in practical application in everyday life situations. I wish for you to find that strength within yourself, to forgive, to love, and to walk the path of truth.

This is just the beginning. More books await you that will deepen your understanding, broaden your horizons, and help you delve further into what it means to be true to yourself and free. In the meantime, I am at your disposal. If you feel you need support, whether through individual or group work, seminars, or workshops, feel free to contact me. Together, we will walk the path of enlightenment.

Know that you are not alone. You are always loved—never, absolutely never, give up on yourself. Your journey of self-discovery, no matter how difficult it may be, leads you to freedom, to love, and to truth.

———◦———

WITH LOVE AND LIGHT,
    Your Alchemist

Copyright Notice: The contents of this book are protected by copyright.

Stefan Stevanovic - Alchemist

Email: tajna.alhemija.uspeha@gmail.com

www.ingramcontent.com/pod-product-compliance
Lightning Source LLC
Chambersburg PA
CBHW052222150726
48002CB00003B/1238